Christening The Coven

Priscilla Mileski

BookLeaf Publishing
India | USA | UK

Made with ❤ on the BookLeaf Publishing Platform
www.bookleafpub.in
www.bookleafpub.com

Dedication

For all the witches past, present and future.

Preface

Again and again the coven forms.

Acknowledgements

Many thanks to the WW Coven, to Madeline, my editor and to Bethany. You keep me motivated, Blessed Be.

1. Christening a Coven

Under your branches,
above your roots, we touch
the beating heartwood of
your elemental core.
Bound, we are the
Coven of the Wylld Willow.
Now and forever more.

2. Mason Jar in Sacred Ground

At the entrance of the path
of the willow tree,
a jar is buried.

Inside, tokens and vows.
A Coven is born of sage, hair,
poetry and icons of love.

Frogs and turtles
of the pond watch from
deep under winter mud.

3. Offerings

Birch bark, corn sheaves
and bird seed. A rune
carved in white driftwood.
Poetry and candles,
herbs and smoke. A
lock of hair from each
coven witch blessed
and bound deep underground.

4. Ode to Einstein the Cat

You helped yourself
to every box, bag, basket
and jacket ever to
enter your house.
You loved a good warm lap.

Our familiar has left us
to always be the shadow
in the hall, the whisker that
flicks in the candlelight.
The soft purr in the night.

5. Hecate's Path

We stop at each
three-way intersection
between our home
and yours. We place coins.
We ask for blessings,
clarity and safe return.
We forge a new
path to the Goddess.

6. Faun

Little Goddess Faun
holds the unknown
with patience and grace.

She sits on the altar
with the jawbone
of the deer whose
death in the field
fed vulture, fox and mouse.

Faun, what do you hold
so luminescent, so dear?

7. Snowdrops for Imbolc

Milk white Snowdrops
rise from the frozen earth.
They capture the radiant
winter sun in their hanging bonnets.
Warmth returns to the Mother
through their tiny bulb roots.

In the low light of morning
Brigid gathers the
young, yearning anemones.

8. Whistle

We call on you Brigid.
Your whistle of warning
sounds the alarm
against anger, greed,
indifference and harm.
We call in the love and
protection of the mother goddess.

Embrace every woman
and the short-lived
innocence of every child.
Help us be the whistle.
To call out corruption
or disruption of the beauty
and sanctity of life.

9. Celebration

That moment, on Imbolc,
after the lighting of the candles,
after the smear of moon-blessed
water on our foreheads,
we fill our brightly
painted ceramic bird whistles
with the magic of water.
We trill in unison -
birds of a coven.
We laugh with joy
to know, we too
can protect Brigid's women.

10. Take Back 2025

It’s early 2025.
More and more women
take back the ancestral craft.
It rises from deep within the belly.
Hecate carries the torch. Salt and sage.
The candle burns.

11. Saturniidae

Luna Moth flutters in her
glorious green gown
for less than a week.
She has no mouth,
no desire to eat.

She has transformed
herself into a goddess solely
to find her mate and lay her
bone-white eggs. She is
every bit a familiar and a muse.

12. Labyrinth

The seed pattern is followed by
concentric rainbow arches,
pencil upon paper, stone upon earth.

The path is clear when we
focus between the lines -
one step at a time.

The center brings us home.
A pause before the turn. Steps retraced
for another try at the beckoning unknown.

13. Green Man

Four new holly trees
along the fence
In the back yard.
Glossy thick leaves and red berries.

They call in the Green Man.
The ancient strength
of the Druids,
the magic of the Holly.

The deeply rooted
magic of the Holly.

14. Sitting With Skunk Cabbage

I've come to sit with
the skunk cabbage.
To breathe in the deep
dark secrets come to light.
Green against brown.
The underground showing us how.

15. Ostara

Sweet tender snowdrops rise and bow.
Daffodils spear upwards to
pierce the sun's warmth.
Preparations for Ostara have begun.

Eggs to color, labyrinths to draw,
candles and gifts. A circle
holds space for laughter and mirth.
A renewal of spirit hangs in the balance.

16. River, Field, Wood

On a mid-day walk.
along the wrack
a bit of driftwood
goes into the backpack.

In the field, a handful
of milkweed left
to blow along the trail.
Grasses bent and broken.

In the wood under fallen trees,
by a well-used burrow
is a bone pile.
A bare jawbone with teeth.

It reminds me to be strong
to be heard, to be remembered.

17. Spring Equinox

We celebrate rebirth, renewal,
new life, balance and the
turning of the wheel.
Rabbits, eggs, bird song.
The return and bloom of color
out of the cold gray earth.

We hold each other up
in strength, with fierce passion,
with hope and action.
We find ourselves
and each other
in the labyrinth of life.

18. April Fool's Day

Only a fool
would miss the crabapple
ready to pop into full bloom,
the serviceberry flowering
white against the blue sky,
the orange and yellow tulips
basking in the sun or
the grape hyacinth gathered
under the budding maple.

I am not that fool.

19. Goddess of Spring

To be a goddess of Spring
don the flowers of May,
dance the maypole.
Bind it with ribbon to
assure new life. Ring bells,
place food for the fae.

Walk between the fire
of the warming sun and the
fire of the seed bursting with life.
Sing the sister songs of
Persephone, Brigid, Freya and Flora.
Wear the gown and the Wylld Willow crown.

20. Sea Witches

On the wild beach of Assateague
the fog rolls in vague and heavy.
Our skin becomes damp.
Our hair grows giddy, crazy with joy.

We are transformed into sea witches.

21. Coffee and Tea

Is the magic
in the spell, the
color of the candle
the reading or the rune?

Or is it in the tea
or the coffee we sip
as we share our words
to the coven story.